Innocence

Innocence

Jean Nordhaus

The Ohio State University Press
Columbus

Library of Congress Cataloging-in-Publication Data
Nordhaus, Jean, 1939–
   Innocence / Jean Nordhaus.
     p. cm.
   ISBN-13: 978-0-8142-5158-4 (pbk. : alk. paper)
   ISBN-10: 0-8142-5158-7 (pbk. : alk. paper)
   ISBN-13: 978-0-8142-9120-7 (CD-ROM)
   ISBN-10: 0-8142-9120-1 (CD-ROM)
   I. Title.
  PS3564.O558I5 2006
  811'.54—dc22

                                     2006015756

Type set in Bembo.
Cover design by Dan O'Dair
Printed by Thomson-Shore, Inc.

9 8 7 6 5 4 3 2 1

To my brother Richard, and in memory of our brother, Ron

. . . he was a true Poet, and of the Devil's party without knowing it.
—William Blake

Contents

III.

IV

Acknowledgments

I wish to thank the following journals in which many of these poems, or their earlier versions, first appeared:

Antioch Review; American Literary Review; American Poetry Review; Chokecherries 2001; Gettysburg Review; Great River Review; Hotel Amerika; Marlboro Review; Natural Bridge; The New Republic; Phoebe; Poetry: "Anniversary," "Earth Music," "From a Window in Jerusalem," "Pauline Is Falling," "Posthumous," "Yiddish," copyrights 1993, 1995, 1997, 1999, 2000 by the Modern Library Association; *Prairie Schooner; Southern Review; Tikkun; West Branch; Window; Yankee.*

Thanks, too, to the following anthologies in which poems from this book were first printed: *The Other Side of the Hill II; An Endless Ribbon of Song: WPFW89.3FM Poetry Anthology.*

"The Rope Was Innocent" and "Yiddish" appeared first in *The Porcelain Apes of Moses Mendelssohn,* Milkweed Editions, 2002.

Special thanks to Mary Ann Larkin, Elaine Magarrell, and Linda Pastan for friendship and helpful suggestions. And to the members of the Capitol Hill Poetry Group for their dedication, week after week, to our common endeavor.

THE ROPE WAS INNOCENT

and the ass, the two man-servants
below on the plain, the ram,
the wood, the knife,
the fire. The pit, the rack,
the bullwhip—all the instruments

were innocent: iron slept
cold in the ground. But love
was not innocent. It was love
who gave the order and love
who obeyed, carried and stacked

the wood, offered wrists and
ankles for the binding. Love
prepared the fire and raised
the knife, and it was love
who lowered it. Bless the animals,

who live without mercy: the ape
with her beautiful breasts
nursing her young, the tethered
ram, and the ass grazing there
in the lowlands—little wooly ass

who cannot pray, who hears only
the braying of wind in the grass
and when death comes with its smell
of lion, answers: Here am I,
and falls to its knees without wonder.

I.

THE INFANT KING

We bring him the best foods,
bundles of embroidered gowns,
soft, soft, a servant

kisses the ruddy feet,
brushes away with leafy fans
the sycophantic flies

flattering the air
around his shoulders.
He has nothing to do all day

but bask in the amplitude
of our affection,
from his throne of batting

to observe the curtains
luffing on currents of air, survey
the troops of grass parading and standing.

Why, then, is he unhappy? Why
does he weep? And why,
if he is indeed a king,

as the idylls of our love
have promised, do we banish him
to his room each night, swaddled

in silence, and dipping him
into the moving dark, consign him
to the vastness of the other kingdom?

I KNEW THE RUDIMENTS

I knew the rudiments: his
into hers. What I lacked
were illustrations. My parents
handed me a solemn book.
It would explain
what they could not. Feverish,
I browsed the chapters ("Eggs,"
"Pollen and Sperm")
past grainy fish roe
(black and white); a nest
of speckled eggs; a flustered
German Shepherd bitch
who nursed her puppies
like the Roman She-Wolf
standing up. All this
I took for metaphor.
Likewise, the sad
fallopian lyre, the bristling
snapdragons, the peacock's
gorgeous poker-hand of plumes.
Only to reach the final
chapter, where an uxorious
bull and cow moose browsed
in a soggy glade, fondling
the ferns with blowzy lips. And *this*,
it seemed, was frenzy's end: the bog,
the weeds, the slow beasts
cumbrous in their bodies.

THE SOUND: *Seventeen Year Cicadas*

The sound was sultry, loud, a steady
sexual hum, swelling, receding, swelling again,
the whole world throbbing like a single animal,
the clumsy creatures, everywhere emerging—winged
beings, monstrous, but gentle, their bodiless shells,
translucent and perfect, littering the walk. Where
was my own sloughed carapace? I stood in my confused
flesh, new breasts budding against my will. The sound
was outside and inside at once—like plunging
into a warm sea not knowing skin from water.

All the next year, I could not get enough
of sleeping, rising briefly, sinking back down—
less depression than a larval lethargy. I lay on the beach,
my new curves nested in sand, heat baking my limbs.
My young brothers buried me. I let them.
They made a long corpse of me, a mummy case.
I barely stirred. I wanted to tunnel down
into the earth, a blind grub burrowing
without sound or thought or music
toward the day when I'd awaken to my winged life.

WAITING FOR A BUS IN BALTIMORE

She is waiting on the corner
in a perfect vacancy of being.
Who do you love? Who do you love?
Her face, like the flat sea on a calm day,
mirroring cloud-drift, mirroring change.

She chews her hair, shifts
her heavy bag from shoulder
to shoulder, gazes out. Her breasts
are round. She is ready.
Who do you love? Who do you love?

A wind from nowhere
raises a litter of pollen and dust.
It swirls about her like a veil.
The stoplight goes from red to green
to red. A bus careens past with a number

not her own. Hers, when it arrives,
will brake with a shriek at her feet,
lower its steps with a shudder of steam.
She will climb aboard, still waiting—
Who do you love? Who do you love? Who?

THE BRUISE

The bruise was grape violet indigo
shot through with veins of chartreuse—
a flower opening, a deep-sea dragon
rising, voluptuous, surprising
to the touch. And her hand
returned to it again, again
as if to plumb its secret. But the bruise
had neither mouth nor breath,
no tongue to tell its double tale
of harm and healing. Over time
the edges yellowed, the swirling
mauves and plums began to fade
so gradually she couldn't say
when it finally slipped away. It was nothing
she needed, nothing the body wanted
but she missed it: the drama, the riot
of color, the tenderness. And often
in the quiet times she felt for it: an absence
on the surface of her smooth unblemished days.

THE NUCLEAR FAMILY

I dream them curbside
near my childhood home, or else
adrift in some unguarded space.
The man could be my husband
or my black-haired father,
a senator, some neighbor
I hardly know. But it's always
the same constellation orbiting
an unseen pole—the bickering children,
the man climbing into a car, the woman,
would-be-mender, wringing her hands
at the edge of the scene. Over time,
they've grown simple and large.
Some nights I am parent; some nights,
child. All that matters is the infinite
unfolding of the comedy, its ritual
enactment, night after night on the road
between anger and love, the great contenders
fixed and moving through a force-field
of opposing longings.

BLUEGRASS

We drive to water Sunday
afternoons through second
growth, rivers of bluegrass
tumbling from the speaker. Trees
thwang past like banjo strings,
the crickets frail. Climbing
with a camera—like carrying
a child or trying out a new,
vulnerable limb, we relearn
the perils of walking,
cautious over rock. The trail
threads downstream, gropes
for water, runs ahead down blind
alleys of rock toward a promise
of green.

       Along the bank,
the rocks lean out and
point upstream like cannon,
single-sighted, while imagination,
edging toward the rim
creeps forward hand by hand
then falters where the heart
drops away like a cliff
to a rope of siltgreen river
twisting in the gorge.

           Hiking home
through spangled woods,
we pass young couples
starting out with ropes.
They will lower themselves
like grasshoppers, just for sport,
over the sheerest cliffs, the ones
we couldn't contemplate
run lightly up and down the strings.

AMBITION

*Hurricane Jean has been demoted to a tropical depression
and is now circling over the Caribbean.*

I'd hoped to make more of a splash, to wade ashore
through tidal waves of acclamation, small boats
bobbing in my wake. Wasn't I the daughter

of contending winds, a child of passionate
engendering? I was the cat's howl. Mayhem
was my middle name. Winding up

for something big, I rattled in my crib
beneath a ceiling of fixed stars. I could have
dumped torrents of rain and sand on the bayous

lifted islands on a single breath, piled them
one over another. Now I must content myself
with smaller gestures: a bucket of water

sloshed over the housing tracts, small creeks
swollen, a tantrum of wind in the hickory groves,
breaking off the damaged limbs, bones already dead.

TWO SIGHTINGS AND A VALEDICTION

This morning's coyote, silver and black
in the sage, her feathery tail afloat.
And last night my old love in the airport
glimpsed for the first time in 28 years—
recognition like a surge of laughter.

I thought to step from the camouflage
of strangers and reveal myself:
I knew his name, but not my own.

Once there were spirits guiding my life.
They brought the fox and the deer
to my window. They brought the moon
to my door. And if he'd come
a moment earlier, a moment later?

Now the sun begins its nightly
valediction. Each weed is blessed. The hills
are glazed with bronze. The clouds continue
what the hills began. They carry it to the sky
to be perfected. Love, do you hear?

I'm sending you a message by that fuchsia cloud,
the one still touched with fire. Do you see it—
in whatever town you landed?

There's a young coyote, curious, shy,
who walks this world in my bones.
The bush she stepped from
shakes with invisible flame,
as I shake in the wind of an earlier life.

WANTING RED HAIR IN OCTOBER

There sleeps at the heart of the world
something heavy and dark,
a she-bear mumbling,

Take off your shoes. Lie down. Come home.

Blood leaps and slows; leaves flare,
then fade and swirl, resistless, down.

Soon the eye will be starved for red,
a cardinal's wing, a berry's fire
against the sky's cold flesh.
                    Ha! Ha! Ha!
The crows are laughing, gravity's
black angels, as they struggle from the ground
and fly away.
        I want to be lifted. I want
red hair, a crimson snatch. I want to blaze
and shimmer like a maple in the wind before the snow
comes visiting with needles full of anesthesia
and I crawl into the cave of sleep and sleep.

THE PLATYPUS DREAMS EIGHT HOURS A DAY

Eccentric as the eyeballs' rumba,
antic as the nerve-strings' fierce arrhythmias
vibrant as the visions bubbling through the brain,
we sail into the shadow-realm like mummies
straight and stiff as Pharaoh gliding
in his death-boat through the underworld.

Joseph and his bending sheaves—
Pharaoh's seven fat and lean—

Not prophesies. Not messages from God.
Not (as some believe) a highway to the ancestors.
Not to help us remember. Not to forget.

Facts:

All mammals dream except the Australian anteater.
The platypus dreams eight hours a day.

Manifesto:

In the end, I refused to evolve. It was
too lovely here among the oozy ferns,
the boggy pools and swamps. How I hated
the harsh light and rough handling,
my mother's blood and martyred privacy.
Better, by far, to be hatched, to roll, untorn
into the world—a clean arrival. To nurse a season
at the milky seeps then slip back
into those quick streams
where everything is magnified and strange—

A dignified department store.
My mother sags, implodes—
Help! she cries. *I need a quack!*—
and I know it's the beginning,
words coming wrong this way.

My daughter, age 3, hair like feathers.
The head, I say. *Be careful of the head,*
She dives into the quarry. Words
like bubbles rising: *Long.*
Narrow. Murky. Deep.

Another quarry. On the edge,
four men in black, hands
bound, about to leap—
A voice, protesting,
But I wanted to live. I loved my life.

When the towers fell,
I could not dream. My single self
with all its flagrant images, its
schemes and reveries slept paralyzed
before the screen, unblinking. Dimmed
to dust and ashes. Pointless all these daily,
small epiphanies: sunlight, apples
on a white cloth, the UPS man
carrying an awkward package
up the steps across the street.

The zoo. I scratch my hand. Blood
flows bright and swift. A platypus
swims up to lick the wound.
By this I know we are blessed
and will live forever.

If death is just another dream,
the last one, will we spend the long

night of eternity dreaming our lives:
childhood's terrors, love's
first rose, flashes of light
on the dark screen? Again. Again. Not
to remember. Not to forget.

Joseph and his bending sheaves
  Endymion among the poppies
    Vishnu, dreaming the world—

II.

I AM TALKING TO YOU ABOUT LOVE

The butcher has gone mad and begun to write.
He has taped a yellow envelope of poems
to his meat-case window with a sign
saying, *Take one.* And if you obey,
you will find yourself collared
by a man with rumpled hair, a cleaver of light
in his pale blue eyes. *See?* He will say.
Do you see? His poems are penciled
in a rough hand, signed like gospel:
Mark, and this is Mark,
who stops you, breathing like a bull
from two soft nostrils, who perspires, who
is talking to you about Love, who is happy,
whose happiness feels like hunger and if you do not
accede on the spot, he might
love you too hard, he might stuff you
back down in the sausage. *Yes.*
In the shadowy meat-case his ham hocks
and knuckles lie bloodless, pale. Voices
have entered this man and fill him
beyond skin's endurance. And now,
you too hear voices: *Back away! Away!*
As you cycle home, a road sign
hollers *STOP.* A bright red canister
left out on your doorstep reads:
IN CASE OF FIRE. For the butcher,
you think. And then, *Have mercy.*

JUNK

On James Hampton's *Throne of the Third Heaven of the Nations' Millennium General Assembly.*
Museum of American Art, Washington, D.C.

Everything begged to be saved:
three-legged tables, arthritic
chairs. The blind light bulbs
and sprung valises longed to be lifted,
transformed. With his dreaming
eye, he saw them as they might become:
the altar wrapped in foil; the gimpy chair
reborn as throne; six twinned pedestals
with flower-faces, strumming brassy music
of the unreal world. And blazoned over all:

Fear Not.

The kingdom of heaven is made of junk.
Busy as a spider in the dim
garage, he built it, fettling forth
winged symmetries and curious
entablatures. A makeshift architecture,
tenuous as a sigh. Here exposed to public view,
it leans away, hoarding its darkness.
No one has appeared to mount the throne,
yet all is readiness. A velvet ribbon
bars the door to the unenterable room.

SURFACE TENSION

Our theme last night was eschatology:
the death of frogs, stampeding asteroids,
the blemishless red heifer of rabbinic lore.

Its ash will cleanse the world
for the Messiah and usher in the end of time—
which some desire. Eccentric chirr

of dinner chatter. Supple, darting tongues.
God hungers for unblemished flesh,
but takes what He can get—like my brother,

who rode to Placid in the jump seat
and never came home. He'd be 51 today.
Teen-driving is our latest form of human

sacrifice. Just check this morning's *Post*—
six in a Subaru Outback. Wild boys.
Out of control. Morning sun. Breeze

on my back. Balance of wildness
and control it takes to make a life,
a work of art, a viable contraption

that will stay afloat. Oh, to ride the secret
waters, dive into the murk and rise
with trophies in my mouth, word-boats

trembling on the surface of the pond—a small
flotilla battling asteroids and global slump,
the absence of frogs or of one boy's life, forever.

THE SAD DREAM OF PEACE

Suddenly one day the fire in all hearts
was dowsed. We set aside our weapons
and embraced our sadness—
not in one room or city,
but in every borough of the world.

The gods with their bristling
spears, their bright helmets and shields,
began to fade—pale images
against the sky, then—
vapor and mist. Lifting our eyes

to the clouds, we saw ordinary things:
a dog, a teakettle. Death came down
and worked among us as an equal
in those denims with the worn out knees.
And dying was easy as setting a cup on a plate.

No dithyrambs. No arias.
Lullabies endured. A few poems.
Soon even these trailed off.
Would the sounds of the near world
be music enough—
    the ruffle of waves against sand,
    a tree limb rubbing
    like a rosined bow across a string?

DINNER ON THE FAULT LINE

It's not the wine that lifts the table so our plates
begin to swim like continents above the heaving
cloth, just this bearded young seismologist talking faults
and slippage—a skinny kid from Flatbush, drunk
on numbers and the rumblings of this unreliable
earth. It will blow soon. Everyone speaks of it.
Some even wish it. And so we goggle half-
believing, like those blubbery disciples etched
by William Blake—more seals than men, a floating
dinner party. Any supper could be the last.

Tomorrow, the earth may roar and swallow us,
our bellies full of grass and shrimp,
or it may keep on, inching forward in small,
digestible hitches, while we walk over it,
erect and warm. Outside the brimming
supermarkets, beggars brandish empty cups
raising their afflictions to our eyes. *Small change.*
Small change. Feasting is a form of prayer.
So rub two sticks together, braise leeks, raise
a soufflé, a little belly-warmth. Let the plates slide.

THE WOODCHUCK

But they don't chuck wood. They dig
holes in the ground until the bank
crumbles into the creek. They are
perfectly useless—
our hostess says, good only
for crab bait. Her husband,
the man in pink trousers,
retreats to the house
and returns with his gun.

We are hilarious with gin
on his lovely veranda (though a girl
with a slender neck
hides her face shrieking, *I don't
believe this*). Understand.
The gun is beautiful,
mahogany, slender,
and shines like all things
burnished with love. And our host
is beautiful, too, all
bronze and silver on his pink
stalks, the one whose land
is crumbling. And the woodchuck
in his shambling way

is only doing what woodchucks
do—digging the earth,
filling his belly, standing
erect like a furry man,
sniffing the hazardous air
with a sensitive nose. Now
he is flat, the spade tail
whipping in circles, and now

just a stain on the lawn.
One of the hairier guests
trots out, belly first,
to remove it. The tail
is a handle, from which hinge

a dangerous hunger
swings. It is not good
to see these matters
always from the victim's
point of view.

And if the windows
rattle like machine-guns
all night long, and I grope my way
by the red-eyed clock
to the bathroom, tracing my dinner
back through all the stations
of the evening till I come at last
to the woodchuck there
on the lawn, will he

pity me here in the dark
as I enter the sight of his infra-red
eye? Will he think me good
only for crab bait? I'm telling you this
because it is late and my dinner
won't go down. The sky
is dark, the moon is
a handle, the gun is beautiful.

IN NAGASAKI

All the boats are bobbing in Nagasaki harbor.
Butterfly is waiting on her hill
for the Americans to come. Her obi

flutters in a breeze that gently stills as if
all breathing in the world had stopped.
And yet the boats bounce gaily in the chop,

waving their colored flags. The tall Americans
will bring appalling news. Butterfly
will bend in grief to meet her knife.

All the boats are gone from Nagasaki harbor.
All the boats and all the water, all the faces
with their names. The Yanks have landed

with their sturdy "can-do," their capacity for harm.
The people of Nagasaki have seen a great light
surrounded by a greater darkness. Here we might pause

to speak of irony, the distance between art
and history, between one woman's harrowing
and holocaust. Such niceties are neither here nor there

to Butterfly. For her, the heart is absolute,
and knowledge means obliteration.
All she needs to know of irony, she knows.

THE LAST ONE

One takes off—who knows why—
just an uneasy feeling. Then two more beat their wings
against the water, kicking to get aloft.
Seeing this, five others change their minds
and decide to go along. Maybe it's not
so safe here. Soon, the whole flock
is taking off in successive waves. The cloud of bodies
fills the air with a whack-whack-whack of wings.
A few stragglers remain—the stubborn, the slow,
the bloody-minded—and now just one,
distracted by a tasty sprat, or an attractive
business opportunity, raises its head
and looks around. Where has everyone gone?
I think of émigrés in dangerous times:
those who leave early—the nervous ones,
the pessimists, the young who can imagine
another life, who haul their sprung valises
onto trains or ships—and others who delay,
snagged in long lines at the embassies
or longer lines along the roads—the ones
who stay too long. One way or another,
all will be leaving. Only a few stay behind,
like those last two Jews in Afghanistan,
who camped together in the ruined synagogue
and did not get along. (*I'm not sorry,*
the younger said, when the old man died.) The last
will leave now too, following the others, wing
by wingbeat on to the next Jerusalem.

YIDDISH

Sometimes when my mother
opened her mouth to speak, a shoe
tumbled out or a featherless
chicken that settled its head
on my pillow, claw-feet
clenched in prayer.

That's when I learned to fear sleep
and to watch the tongue for danger,
to throw scraps of paper
over the rail and watch
them fall, each fluttering
word, a white dove.

Now I pluck them back
and bury them until
they bloom again on the tip
of my tongue and rhyme:
The kiss and the pillow.
The tree and the plum.
A house built of wood

and others, like stanzas, a village
of stanzas. A school. A bridge.
The song running under it. Quick
as a scale. The *sofer*'s long
black coat turned inside out,
patched with diminutives,

basted with stitching
of every color. I try it on.

It fits me perfectly.
The syllables fit in my mouth
like smoke in the chimney,
like milk in a thimble,
the child in its grave.

TO HOLD

Before I left for camp, my mother sewed my name
with a firm stitch into everything I owned.
She even looped a string of nametapes
through the scissors I keep to this day on my desk.

She wanted to be sure, when she sent me into the woods,
she'd get the right child back at summer's end,
that I'd not be left in the laundry drum
like an unmarked sock. Others—

careless, lazy mothers—favored marking pens,
illegible black letters bleeding into stain.

My mother knew nothing was permanent.
She'd seen how fast a child could disappear:
her two dead sisters with names like flowers:
Lily, Rose, their summery smells, indelible voices.

That's why she sewed my name so tight
on all four sides, double-knotted the knots.
So I wouldn't forget when she sent me off
into the wet, the dark, the wild: I was hers.

AUNT LILY AND FREDERICK THE GREAT

After the war, she painted her walls
a French blue, pale as the watered
blue silk of her eyes, filled her rooms
with cream and gold-leaf chairs,
and when she raised her porcelain cup
with pinky arched and blew the word
"Limo-o-o-ges" across the lip,
that made a tender wind, as if a host
of cherubs rafted through the room.
Mad for all things French,
she'd never read Voltaire,
went straight from the Academy
of Typing in the Bronx to work
for Mr. Hyman at the J.D.C.
In 1945 she went to Paris—ah, the city
was a shambles then, American cigarettes
were currency, her Yiddish
far more useful than her French
for working with the refugees. History
was hell, she learned, but life
moved on. She purchased
silver fruit knives, teacups, pastel
figurines, and tottered home on platform
wedgies to attend the rattle and attack
of morning trucks along Third
Avenue and to receive us kindly
when we came to call—in short,
to lead a life not *sans souci*
(for there were deaths,
and loneliness), but of her own
design. You'd never guess
King Frederick and my aunt
would have so much
in common. Both were short,
bilingual, stubborn, confused,
enlightened in some ways, benighted
in others, tyrannical, clever, benevolent,
fierce. Like Frederick, she flourished,
like Frederick, she died. She was tiny
and great and is buried in Queens.

ANNIVERSARY

I remember the heat, the green-striped tent,
the little canapes of crab and ham,
my frazzled mother, guests in summer hats,
bowls of roses wilting on the tables,
and how the water fell upon the ground
as rain and rose again. There was a body there
impersonating me. It wore my face,
my ice-blue linen dress (I had refused
the white) and stood, benumbed, on ice-blue
linen spikes while kisses floated by
like ducks along a moving track.
I felt that I was living
someone else's life, surprising
as the wedding presents heaped upstairs,
those pristine bowls and implements whose uses
I could barely guess. And you, so cheerful,
there beside me, wanting this.
We hardly knew each other then, although
our bodies recognized each other well enough
and half-suspected they could live together.
Were the day and the hour propitious?
Many who now are gone were still alive.
Others had not yet arrived. The auguries
said neither yes nor no, but there was water
in the air and on the ground and I
have held you in my arms as air
holds water to relinquish it again.

III.

THE WHITE MEAL

Lord, give us food for angels and invalids,
poets and madwomen, all who find
the savor of this world too strong—
mourners and saints and those volatile souls
whose joy ignites dangerous fevers; for these
a cloud, a polished bone, a cup of snow
is sustenance enough. Spread them a tablecloth

clean as the page of an unwritten book
and serve upon crockery
plain as a nurse, the clear broth
of memory, skim milk of exile,
cooked grains and potted cheeses, purées
shred from pale roots, breast-meat,
slivered from the bony tent.

Let this feast be lean as Pharaoh's
seven dream-cows, humble to bless
the blue feet of the starving and let
each vessel, passed from hand to hand
above our plates, inscribe a circle
over circles. Let no clamorous spice,
no storm of seasoning distract these diners

from their secret craving—to hear
a mother's tongue toll again
in the rhythms of childhood, see steam
rising from the earliest soup, sunlight
flashing from a spoon, raised—
as lighthouse over waves—
a beacon for the hungry voyager.

TO TELL A SORROW

My mother's in the ICU, she says
as she takes my hand, sets it
in a blue ceramic dish to soak,
And my father's got dementia, studies
the mangled quick, the gnawed cuticles.
Ammoniac of hair-dye, attars of acetone
and mousse—something in the air
inspires disclosure. *Don't tell!*—I feel
my mother's arm around my neck,
my brother's palm, a gag of bone,
across my lips. *Don't throw us in a beggar's grave
with others' griefs.* But all around us
women unravel their worries, gorgons in rollers
and lettuce-green gowns ogling the mirrors in horror
and hope. Oh, to be golden, exempt: *La belle
Hélène,* imperious Isolde. The idylls of the beautiful
roll on forever. And who am I to hold myself aloof—
addict of compromise, ripe for revision?
I give her my flayed nails, my ragged cuticles,
and hand in hand, before the gaudy tiers
of bottles, every bubbled shade of glitz and shame,
we sing our sorrows to the listening, complicit air.

A DANDELION FOR MY MOTHER

How I loved those spiky suns,
rooted stubborn as childhood
in the grass, tough as the farmer's
big-headed children—the mats
of yellow hair, the bowl-cut fringe.
How sturdy they were and how
slowly they turned themselves
into galaxies, domes of ghost stars
barely visible by day, pale
cerebrums clinging to life
on tough green stems. Like you.
Like you, in the end. If you were here,
I'd pluck this trembling globe to show
how beautiful a thing can be
a breath will tear away.

PAULINE IS FALLING

        from the cliff's edge,
kicking her feet in panic and despair
as the circle of light contracts and blackness
takes the screen. And that
is how we leave her, hanging—though we know
she will be rescued, only to descend
into fresh harm, the story flowing on,
disaster and reprieve—systole, diastole—split
rhythm of a heart that hungers

only to go on. So why is this like my mother,
caged in a railed bed, each breath,
a fresh installment in a tortured tale
of capture and release? Nine days
she dangled, stubborn,
over the abyss, the soft clay crumbling
beneath her fingertips, until she dropped
with a little bird cry of surprise
into the swift river below.

Here metaphor collapses, for there was no love
to rescue her, no small boat
waiting with a net to fish her out,
although the water carried her,
and it was April when we buried her
among the weeping cherries and the waving
flags and in the final fade, a heron
breasted the far junipers
to gain the tremulous air and swim away.

POSTHUMOUS

Would it surprise you to learn
that years beyond your longest winter
you still get letters from your bank, your old
philanthropies, cold flakes drifting
through the mail-slot with your name?
Though it's been a long time since your face
interrupted the light in my door-frame,
and the last tremblings of your voice
have drained from my telephone wire,
from the lists of the likely, your name
is not missing. It circles in the shadow-world
of the machines, a wind-blown ghost. For generosity
will be exalted, and good credit
outlasts death. Caribbean cruises, recipes,
low-interest loans. For you who asked
so much of life, who lived acutely
even in duress, the brimming world
awaits your signature. Cancer and heart disease
are still counting on you for a cure.
B'nai Brith numbers you among the blessed.
They miss you. They want you back.

THE STONES WERE MUTE

I went to look for you
in April where I'd seen you
last, but the earth slammed shut. I found
three stone plaques, three doors
in the earth. I knocked. The stones
were mute. Cars moaned past
on the Interstate. The high
voltage lines were keening.
Even the weeping cherries
were sham—a fleck
of blood inside each ruffled
blossom. Beautiful grief,
where have you gone? Why do I
walk this world like a sleep-walker
while the dead wait with their knuckles
clutched over their breastbones,
refusing? The animal gods
have slithered back into the kiva
smoke hole, pulling the lid closed behind.

FROM A WINDOW IN JERUSALEM

Light returns to the stones
as blood to flesh, suffusing
the walls. I watch the cold city
revive and think of
my own dead. Even before we put
them in the earth, the bones
began to crumble in their bodies.
Now they walk my feet
over stony hills, clamber
in and out of busses, sample
this world through my pores.
Whatever food I taste,
I taste for you. Of this guilt, too,
I absolve myself. Only the absence
remains, so huge
it is wordless. I begin to rock
as the pious do, for grief
and prayer and gratitude, one motion
welling in the body. Now the birds
fly up, and I know
that all the dead since time
began have risen—the graves
in the yard below are empty. The sun
breaks free from a blindfold of cloud
to hang on the hill above Gehenna,
swollen and round as a ghost
balloon, one of the streetlamps
left on from my childhood
still shining at dawn.

EACH DAWN'S BREAKING

For one last night these walls
will settle like a robe around my shoulders.
I'll reenter childhood's rooms, exhume
the darkness under cellar stairs
and hear my father calling.

I will stand on the spot
where the apple tree stood
to feel its amputated stump
flower again with the bodies
of children, sway with Schubert

in the long room half-lit
by the yellow heron-lamp
on the piano, while the night–
beast presses his enormous hide
against the panes—

I'll lie once more in my bed
under water-blue walls,
watch the red-eyed radio towers
blinking down the line like fingers
drumming on a table,

rise again to the north-light
of childhood, days so bleak
I wept to wake, knowing this world
forsaken from the womb, each dawn's
breaking, rehearsal for this one.

MY MOTHER LIES HEAD TO HEAD
WITH ESTHER STONE

My mother lies head to head
with Esther Stone.
My brother and father
with Jacob Rose
and one whose name
is not yet inscribed.
What do they talk about
all night with total
strangers in this frozen
suburb of the soul? The seasons
have done what they can,
mounding the soil on my mother's grave
to mimic the cushion of flesh.
I brush wet leaves aside to touch
the letters of my brother's name
and find raw earth still
bleeding at the borderline
where bronze cuts into sod.

ELDERLY WOMAN HOLDING A DEAD BIRD
SURREY COUNTY ASYLUM, CIRCA 1855

Straw hat, skimpy braids, a checkered dress—
on her face, that knowing look the simple wear
to mask incomprehension. She holds the bird
in her lap like a limp corsage,
the dangling neck, a spill of feathers—light
spilling over the dam of her hands.

Once I played ball with a kitten, with my friend
Gus tossed it, till the neck hung
strange, and red juice trickled from
the small, pink nose. I wrapped my hands
around its soft, gray middle and ran to my
mother please fix it fix it she could not

Eight years old, I hold on my unwilling
lap this writhing worm of flesh,
my brother—on my face, a look of puzzled
sorrow at the world's injustice which has
pinioned me under the glare
of my father's twin lamps, hot and white

as a reprimand. That look
will stare from a frame
in childhood's vestibule forever
rippling in the underwater
chandelier-light, amber shadows
shivering across my face like nervous fish.

The father with his Roloflex, the brother
who, at 18, stepped into an idling
car, the sorrowful mother
drowning in her bones—
if the bird had life it could sing of these
and staple them to the page:

> I be this woman/girl this one this knowing
> only that the flown be still and move
> not flutter not and caused it I did
> not know what knot-wings my shoulder-
> stumps and broken at the neck like
> this one warbling in my lap all wrong—

She hobbles from the frame,
a bird herself (come barely
to my chest) and sets the heap
of feathers in my willing hands
which trembling take
as if to give it life.

ARROYO SECO: A HOUSE AT THE CROSSROADS

Everyone stops here
but not for me. My low house
of earth and water

hunches in a ditch, its windows
sealed against the cold.
Through sheets of plastic over glass

becoming sand, tall mountains
wobble across the tableland
like wandering

gods of an old religion,
snow-haired, robed in blue.
Each afternoon the sun-boat

slides across the southern sky
more swiftly, leaving in its wake
a ruin of purple smoke. At night,

the sky runs clear again, as rivers clear
after a massacre of fish. *Solstice*
over *solitude* leaves *solace*—

words as sustenance, the heart
a simple syllable, a beat.
Nine months beyond my mother's death,

I pause at the door
between freedom and grief and wait
for the future to come.

The herald arrives as an owl
on a dead tree, swiveling
its head, facing backward

and forward at once, as the shadow
of mullion and leaf on a white-
washed wall, the rumbling

approach of an engine. Heart, do you hear
how it slows at the crossroad, falters,
then catches and goes on?

THE MOUNTAIN

Those Tewa girls playing soccer
in the photograph beside my desk
must be nearly grown by now,
black hair shining. By now they wear
the ready, expectant look
of pilgrims entering the promised land,
sloughing off the sleep of childhood
to make their dwelling in the heart's domain.
Some may have children themselves by now.

The mountain, meanwhile, has hardly changed
and I can see how those who have lived always
in its shadow might grow sad to be reminded—
by its steady crown, its rock indifference
to vagaries of light, wind, clouds—
how easily their own lives swirl away
   quick as a jackrabbit running the road
   swift as a silver fish swimming the gorge
   shadowy as the coyote, slipping back into the sage
     never the same one twice

and maybe the mountain, set in stone
above their roofs and lives, would wish
if it could wish, to be like these,
to slip its fixed dominion, enter
the mutable world and float away
   to go noisily like the river
   silently like the weasel, like the field mouse
   taken by the hawk, the hawk
   taken by the wind.

IV

EARTH MUSIC

The Golden Age of Chinese Archaeology
National Gallery, Washington, DC

Pottery Urn with Incised Pictographs

She looms by the entry in half-light,
a vessel the shape of a shawled woman,
guarding enigmas. Battered and crazed
as the moon, she may have held
millet, or wine, or a man, or his ashes.
She may have squatted by the hearth
for ages, waiting to be lifted,
filled. On the curve of her belly:
a map of first things—*Fire, Mountain,
Sun.* How it was before words.

Oracle Bone: Inscribed Scapula of an Ox

The mouth is wet, articulate, but it's the bone,
scraped clean and dry, that holds the delicate
incisions. This one, broad and flat as a spade,
reads: *offer to ancestress Yi a fine pig,
to ancestress Gui a boar, to ancestress Ding
a pig* . . . And who are these ancestral
gluttons, still hungry even down there?
Little speech-bone, shovel-blade
carrying loam between their lives
and ours, tell me—*How shall we feed our dead?*

My Father Did Not Believe

My father did not believe in an afterlife.
My children are my immortality, he'd say.

Parlous inheritance, though thinking so
enabled him to go with grace when death
arrived and little fuss. Over time, his features
thinned and sweetened. He grew transparent
as a winter moth and slipped away, leaving to us
his love of language and his heavy bones,
his melancholy and his brief euphorias, deep
legacy committed to our mortal keeping.

Tomb of Marquis Yi of Zeng

Grievous to give it all up: color, pattern,
texture, taste; the smell of earth, the touch
of hands. Egregious to take it along,
the ample house, its halls and chambers
echoed underground. If he must dive
into that nether world, then all he loves
of this must come along—chairs,
chalices; clothing, victuals; servants,
concubines, even the dog. A dread contingent.
Not to go alone into that kenneled dark.

Chime of Twenty-six Bronze Bells

Bring the bells down. Let their hollows
fill with loam, the long vibrations
undulating through the layers, a rhythm
deeper than our own, beyond all hearing.
Earth music. Ten thousand years would not suffice.
And you? Abandoned in that region from which none
return, what music would you bring along?
    —The wind, not the instruments, the wind
    among the yellow leaves and memory,
    that goes on ringing in the brain's deep passageways.

As for the Dog

As for the dog, with her mottled fur,
her amorous nose, her wet, imploring eyes,
and feral ways—suppose she was not
wrenched away before her time,
but left to doze a winter longer
by the fire, a hand scratching her belly
while her hind leg measured time.
Perhaps she heaved a last great sigh
of happiness, and after was admitted
to her master's tomb, in final debt of fealty.

Jade Shroud Sewn with Gold Wire

Less a king's garb than the molted carapace
of some strange insect, mimicking the shape
of man. Whatever houses here, cocooned
in jade, the man is gone. Only something of his wish
remains: to continue, at all cost, to be. Place a pearl
in the royal mouth. Plug eight openings to keep
self in, corruption out, jade codpiece cupping
the beloved penis. Sleep, now, long and gently
in these hard pajamas. Dream of waking
with a perfect body, beautiful as sin and incorruptible.

My Mother, Likewise

My Mother, likewise, had no trust in immortality.
No metaphor or metamorphosis could comfort *her*.
To come again as grass or bee, a turn of phrase
in someone else's mouth held no appeal. Literal,
and fierce as any mandarin, she wanted meat
and fragrance, flesh and flame, the marrow
and the gist. Hence her tenacity, her Gordian grip.

Her mouth turned down as if she tasted something bitter
and though I offered tender custards, consommés
and sugared violets, I could not appease her hunger.

Pity the Poor Silks

Pity the poor silks, immured in the ground.
And praise the desecrators, digging with fine spoons
in unforgiving earth, who raised them to the light.
The dead are angry. They are not at peace.
These priceless jades, immortal bronzes
are no use to them. They envy us
our life on earth, and nothing we can do or say
assuages. A fine pig, a carved stone, a deathless
eulogy. They would exchange all this and more
to feel again the touch of rain, the brush of silk
on skin, the first faint pricking of appeasable desire.

Bronze Cooking Vessel

How, then, to leave? With fanfare and trumpets?
A tolling of bells? With wailing? With words?
There are no words. However acclaimed or beloved,
they have entered silence, and out of great silence
may come some small thing. A cooking pot, say,
with a chamber for charcoal, its door handle—
a tiny man, his left foot severed for some crime.
They've made him gatekeeper—A crude
exchange: The damaged sentry cannot run away.
He guards the entry faithfully, because he has no choice.

THE INNOCENT

Alone and together, we stand on the platform
a mob of strangers awaiting a train. There may be
among us a wife-beater; surely, a thief. That man
in the blue dolphin tie; that frazzled woman,
gathering in her scattered girls; each of us caught
in the swill of our being; none of us blameless,
not one of us pure. Greedy, covetous,
selfish, vain, we have trafficked in lies; we
have practiced small cruelties. Even the baby,
asleep in a sling on his mother's breast,
has been willful, has shaken with rage.

Yet, if fate arrives, as a wind, in a bullet,
a bomb, at the instant of shock, in the silent
heart of conflagration, we will all
be transformed into innocents, cleansed
in the fires of violence, punished not for any sins
committed—but for standing where we stand,
together in the soft, the vulnerable flesh.